# SPEAK TRUTH BE POWER

# SPEAK TRUTH
# BE POWER

BY MAGICK ALTMAN

Other works by Magick Altman

*Magick Tarot: A Journey of Self-Realization*
*Magick For The Earth, CD*

Copyright © 2020 by Magick Altman
All rights reserved. This book or any portion thereof may not be reproduced or used in any manner whatsoever without the express written permission of the publisher except for the use of brief quotations in a book review.

Published by *Magickal Times Books*

Cover Art by Devin Yakoushkin
Book Design by Sofía Limón
All rights reserved. Used by permission.

ISBN 978-0-9979416-1-6

*For my daughters Celeste, April and Allegra, my grandchildren Devin, Sareen and Phoenix and our extended tribe. You have given my heart wings to fly towards freedom for us all!*

## CONTENT

Mother Revolution / 8
At Blackberry Time / 11
We Are Becoming Wild Again / 14
My Time Of The Month / 18
If I Am The Only Holy / 22
Daylighting The Water Daughter / 28
Spill The Beans / 32
Hail Mary / 35
Fog Is A Definite State Of Mind / 39
Dancin' In The Reign Of Terror / 45
Such An Old, Old Woman / 48
I Am Death, I Am Life / 54
The River / 58
Alice Walker / 62
Halima Khalif Ibrahim / 66
Audre Lorde / 68
Justice For Andy / 72
Justicia Para Andy / 76
Corona Cocoons / 79
The Year Of The Phoenix / 84
Parliament Of Owls / 86

*April Faith Hirschman wrote this poem for me one Mother's Day. I am opening my book with her words so you may know who I am through the eyes and words of my daughter who truly sees me.*
*I am both humbled and honored.*

## MOTHER REVOLUTION
## FOR M.A., LOVE APRIL

She travels in local circles that spiral her
Into the Universe
The Universal
In a moment she shifts from rose petal
innocence to the fierceness of sudden fire

Her Amazon calling carrying her to Haight Street in its blazing days. To the edges of defiance contrary to war. Never choosing comfort when there is someone being unspoken for.

To the mountains along the pyramids she climbs and to the peaks of San Francisco

Bare feet along Civic Center streets
chanting loud to bring about a quiet
peace again. Same place. Different Decades.

Same desire for a sane world.  Different faces.
Through her eyes she sees a world revolving
dancing back into itself.
She skates along Dawns of Aquarius. She dives under
to consult with the depths of the seven seas
This spark cannot be caught in a bottle
This bird flying backwards.
Linking past and present with daisy chains
This eagle resting in Egypt
Rising up in Rome
This eagle presiding over the civil revolutions
the Americas plunged into.
So many freedoms to forage
for so many people's dreams.

Scraping the rust of decadent prejudices
off the arches of rainbows.
The 1960's vision rippling in concentric circles
to like-minded continents.
Funneling the song through revolution's currency:
music, dance, sensual expression, cries of freedom, crying out
for the sake of joy.
The beat catching on in
Europe, in Africa, in small ways in smaller villages.
You pick up the thread through the Occupy
Movement weaving it along the Continuum of
Change.

Living out a life as a quest, a talisman handed to you at birth.
The torch was passed to you fair lady and you dazzle in its glow.

## *AT BLACKBERRY TIME*

Impatient plucking
brings a tart tang to my mouth.

The best ones give themselves to me,
   with gentle fingers they come
        falling off the vine,
So ready, so willing to be tasted.
Plump, black in the burning Sun
They are flush, full, and I just know
    how  sweet  they  are.

The surging juices let loose a festival of flavor,
     Lips held close,
         now painted like a Lady of Night,
       cannot restrain the mmm's and ah's -
Licking purple finger tips,
I reach for more.

This time, my first time, this season,
I bring no bucket to collect her jewels
for baking or freezing for the winter,
No, this time I just want to duck in and out
between her tangled arms
and savor the Queen of summer[1]'s charms.

Sometimes she grabs me
      with her thorns and pulls me close...
   I am teased by the dangerous chance of pain
Breathing deeply,
  I venture in again.

No one can take her sweetest treasures,
I can only yearn to reach into the thorny heights and depths of her
protected pleasures.
There's one above me dying to be eaten-
I hope a blackbird finds her first
                          before
The sun shrivels up her skin and she grows old.
      but no sadness now.

I am humbled by her power to protect herself from us,
We have been too greedy so many times
      when there has always been enough.

                      ...Sated, I walk on
To see other humans
painting themselves in her purple passion,
  unabashed and blissful
                As a baby at its Mother[1]'s breast.

Blackberries bedeck the paths and parks and even roadsides,
  dusty from the spinning wheels of our hurried lives,

but still they thrive.
No one feels like they're stealing,
                         At Blackberry Time,

An unspoken remembering surfaces;
            a deep genetic knowing
                    that we own nothing.

We are her children once again, feasting on her bounty,
           It feels so good
          to know
                There's still something
            we all share.

## WE ARE BECOMING WILD AGAIN

We are becoming wild again
roaming
the streets of the walled cities
demanding justice,

We are becoming wild
refusing to obey, to submit
to accept the lies,
Refusing to let ourselves
be imprisoned by our fears
Our fears will make us all the more ferocious!

We are like tigers pacing on the freeways
stopping traffic, stopping the machine
we are the elephants stampeding
to rescue our children
from the jaws of death.

We are snarling in our hunger for justice
we are like sharks ready to devour
anyone that will pollute the waters of the Earth.

We are wild animals refusing
to believe that anyone owns
the body of the great mother
we are roaring like lions,

screeching like owls with ancient wisdom
that the laws of man
are a trick to protect thieves
and tyrants
and we are wild animals
Declaring our allegiance to the Earth
to Earth Justice
to the laws of nature,
that love is power
that there is more life in a single
petal of a rose then ever pulsed through
the hearts of dictators and military generals.

So many police have become thugs
and criminals, putting our brothers and sisters
in prisons
in the name of progress and profit.

We will break down
the gates to the dark factories
where children labor from dawn
to dusk to feed the economy.

We will laugh like hyenas
in the face of fascism,
shake our rattles like snakes
hissing and slithering through
the halls and malls,

where they sell her body
in little plastic packages
that smell of death.

We are becoming wild again
and we will fly with the eagle that refuses
to be used as a symbol of war any more.

When we destroy the dams
We will once again understand the language
that comes out of the mouths of rivers,
We will converse with the spirits of the rain forests
 as we drive out the oil drillers that are pillaging paradise.

We will tie the likes of the Koch brothers
and the Walton family to the mighty oaks
and have them take magic mushrooms
until all they want to do is hug trees, beg for mercy
and sing hymns of praise to the Great Mother!

We are becoming wild again, and the laws of the universe
will protect us-
The law that love conquers all
that there is nothing more fierce
then a mother wolf fighting for the lives of her cubs,

We are gathering in herds, swarming like bees, out in the open,
we will not hide, only to be hunted down and picked off
one by one.

We have all been in the cages of zoos
too long, waiting to become extinct,
we had almost forgotten
that humans come from humus
we are re-rooting ourselves in this black Earth,

Because black is beautiful Oh! Mother Africa!
We remember now where we came from
we are wild women, wild warriors,
when words fail
we will howl and cry and wail and scream
and stomp our feet!

We are becoming wild again
and freedom never tasted so good!

## MY TIME OF THE MONTH

It's my time of the month-
    Deep emotions
Spill out with the blood-
....I cannot catch it!
Didn't mean to make a mess,
didn't expect to say all this...

But life is raw in its beginning,
    Subtlety is not yet spinning,
I cannot tell you why I feel,
    Only that I know its real.

So many veils have hidden me,
    woven of fear and stupidity,
My eyelids fall from ingrained shame,
    Don't you want to know my name?

Kali dances black and torrid,
    While the truth it is all too horrid,
Women burn on their husband's pyre,
    It is safer to be a proper liar.
Pain stays hidden behind the eyes,
(while proper ladies tell comforting lies)
Yet I fail to see the purpose
of feelings kept below the surface.

Arab women hide their faces,
Jewish women hold their places,
American women act like men,
Stereotypes demean us all,
Can't we be ourselves again?

Hindu women bought and sold,
Asian women never bold,
Latinas become imitation Marys
The Black woman takes all the weight
                she can carry,

What is this burden called womanhood?
   I hate to do what I should!
The gift of life is not a sin,
What is this battle men must win?

What is this fear that makes us mean,
   That makes us think that blood's unclean?
Do you think man you'll lose your role,
   If we women achieve our goal?

As the modern world pulls us together,
We must try to learn to weather
   All this close-knit alienation,
And find in ourselves a new revelation,

That men and women are not at war;
   You're not the bastard,
     I'm not the whore!
We could give each other so much more
   if we'd open understanding's door.

The mysteries I have to speak,
   They cannot come from the passive and weak,
We must know that feelings are strong,
   Feelings give harmony to life's song.

   It's my time of the month,
      I must confess,
   Should that be my excuse
      for saying all this?

As the waves come over me
   the oracle opens my mystery,
I cannot help but say what I see,
We must rescue our humanity.

   To be horrified again at death,
     (to stop whispering under our breath)
   To stop averting our guilty eyes
      when hunger is caused by guilty lies.

We must handle this fear
   of each other's power,
   to let all humanity begin
to flower!

It's my time of the month,
It's my time of the year,
It's my time of the age!
   So wake up, Dear!

## *IF I AM THE ONLY HOLY*

If I am the Only Holy,
If I am good, pure,
    saintly,

Who is going to be evil
    for me?
If I am a sun-worshipping,
   Rational, sane, normal
     Woman,

Who is going to howl
   At the moon
   And dance madly
    When she is full
     Before me?

If I can logically accept
  The cruel reason
    For the Emperor's
       Righteous war,
Who will be the Fool
  And
      Smiling place
      The daisy
In the barrel
  Of the rifle?

If I am to Spiritually
        Transcend
This messy life
And reach
        Nirvana
        Samadhi
        Heaven,

Who will remember
  The trees are sacred,
    That stagnant,
      Smelly swamps
    Must be protected
      As the very wombs
        Of life.

If I cannot
  Own my shadow
Take the dark journey
  That will lead me
    To scream
    In outrage
That we are killing our
    Mother
Our Earth
Our ancient Self,

Who will be there
   To partake
      Of the ritual of life?

I wish to wear no wings
   And do not pray for him to save me,

Am no Angel
  For I have lived and Lusted,
Laughed
   And lost it all

Only to find myself
  Bruised and broken
    A cracked vessel

Still aching to hold to life-
   To be filled
      With life
     With love.

I have been
   Etched with lines

Gone round in circles,

Lost my way
   A million times,

I am a character

   Scarred by my initiations
Proud to own my pain.
   I am stained
      With blood
Poisoned by pesticides,

Shamed by the lies
   I tell myself
To get thru each day-

Knowing I am part of
    The
       Genocide
Against species
   I cannot
      See are
Sown into the
      Fabric that
       Is my own.

I am an
   Extinguisher-
I am the Executioner
I am the cause
     Of extinctions
     For species
A billion years old,
And I refuse to

Pretend
That religion
Means anything-

Unless it means
Love of every
Petal,
Peacock,
Pond,
Yes! And every girl/woman
Guardian
Of the door
Between the worlds,

Who shall never be raped
Again,
Or forced to bear
New life
That no one will help
Her Nurture,
I will not participate
In that future.


I am good
And I am evil,
So do not try to tell me
Sell me

      Sainthood,
Tell me to
   Be good,
I will own my evil
   No separate personified
          Devil
       Scapegoat
         Footnote
   For your God,
I Am Accountable
   For all of me,
And
   I am ready
     To reroot myself
In this dirty Black
     Earth
Anyone who doesn't
   Like it here
   Can leave.

*From Seattle, Washington to Seoul, South Korea, daylighting of creeks is becoming a worldwide effort. The goal is to restore a stream of water to its natural state, which has previously been diverted into a culvert, pipe or drainage system.*

*It is time to free the waters of the world!*
*Daylighting is one piece of the process.*

## DAYLIGHTING THE WATER DAUGHTER

Some say, what's done is done,
Some say she just babbled anyway,

But listen closer.
Silence your mind, put your ear to the ground,
You can hear her pounding against her cement ceiling,
Begging to be heard.

Some say, what's done is done,
Her pores stuffed with gravel
From the last time
The gavel of injustice fell,
And few who live remember
Her anguished cries
As they sentenced her to hell.

What's done is done, they say,
Build 5 stories, maybe ten,

Upon her liquid skin,
Her kind shall not be seen again.
She rumbles and paces
Her cries, now only mumbles,

But, one day, she knows
Her mother will
Shake out the seemingly solid surface,
Forming a mouth for her living river,
So she may burst forth shouting, I am free!
Her ecstatic cries echoing to the mountaintops,
As she erupts, a geyser steaming, with furious force,
From her prison underground!
The sun hits her body like
Lightning from thunder clouds,
And she knows again her heavenly sister's touch
As raintears of reunion
Bless her shimmering skin!

The winds and willows guide
Her course languishing for a moment
in her Laguna lover's arms,
She gains strength,
And rushes on down the river
To her very source!
Mother ocean greets her
 at Jenner with the cries of gulls,

The yelps of seals, Kites and hawks hover
Overhead, Yemaya pounds the beach with
Wave after wave, of welcome,

Embracing the patient one,
The faithful one,
Who always knew she was innocent,
Who always knew she was beautiful,
That she did not deserve to be locked
Away in a cold cement channel
That crushed her curvaceous body,

That starved her of sunlight
That kept her from the joy of suckling the little ones
with their first drink of liquid love,

And yet, like Kuan Yin, she pours her compassion out
upon the world,
And forgives even the faithless city fathers,
Calling them all to slake their thirst and remember
That they are water, too, that their body is her body,
is the eagle's body,
As he soars to the heavens to declare her liberation,
And the egrets take flight, fifty at time,
And the frogs croak, and the crows caw
To let her know she was never forgotten,

The souls of the Miwok and the Pomo
Rise in her mists, chanting and wheeling in circles.

The grandmothers take axes
And rip the granite from her banks,
To let the earth breathe and grow green again,

The children come to plant willows and reeds,
And seed a garden by her shore
Giving her all the love she needs to recover, discovering
their reflection in her water
They greet the daylight daughter and dance!

## SPILL THE BEANS

I've decided to tell all
  Somebody has to,
                Spill the beans
To grow the beanstalk
              Reach the heights
              Battle the demon
          And win!

Time is of the essence
        And the essence is love.
Her scent is everywhere:
        The existence of everywhere
Is the power of her scent.
                Nose to Rose
                  The Universe explodes
                        Into Beauty!
People ask one another-
        Do dreams have any meaning?
Revealing cryptic pieces of the whole.
        Dreams do come true
           Imagination predates the image
        And by creating it, dates it.

What if we believed our dreams
        Before they came true?
Would truth become dreamlike
        And all dreams true?
All perspective pronouncedly different.

If at all possible
  We best dream true now,
For this hellish nightmare
  Of war, rape, famine,
    greed, disease, and
              debauchery,
Is a bad, bad movie
  played on an old
      and broken projector.

Time to direct
  Our lives Toward living
Before our lies and doublespeak
Negate our very existence:
  We are cancelling ourselves
    out of the equation of life.
        Two=Zero
  Duality is both limitation
        and
  Infinite possibilities
  One of which is death.

We are caught by
The Emperor, Sky God King
A spoiled brat with all his things
    Careening down the
highway
    In his Chariot of Strife.
Come on down, Sky God,
    Get your ass on the
ground
Feel, Understand, Caress
    The Great Round

The mysterious Birthplace
  that makes our hearts pound
Beating out Rhythms
  Ecstatic, Alive,
It is life that is Sacred
For what do we strive?

Come home, People
Worship Mother
Choose Life!

## HAIL MARY

I was walking by a church one day
        it was nearly the twilight hour,
A gust of wind blew open the door,
And the light of the votive candles
         drew my eyes to the sterile room.

An old woman was kneeling
        and whispering prayers
Before the Virgin Mary.
I pulled my coat against the cold,
        and tried to hurry on,
But the statue's sad and lonely stare,
Called my soul to enter there.

As I walked in,
        to my amazement,
                 The statue came alive!
Tears were falling from her face,
        She looked into my heart,
And Mary's voice both trembling,
        And infinitely kind
Spoke as if inside my mind.

"I want to leave this place!" she said,
"I cannot breathe,
        I have no life,

No one understands me here,
The people come because they fear
    The wrath of a jealous god.

I miss my sisters, where is Artemis,
Athena, Isis, Kali?

The stories they tell about
        the brilliant Eve,
That the knowledge of life,
        she used to deceive,
Denies the initiation we all must receive,
    To live a life of truth.
And then there's Ruth
    and the Magdalene,
Treated like a whore obscene,
When I know she is a Priestess.
I want all those priests
    To now confess,
        Take off their skirts
            and their crucifixes
And clean up this ugly mess!"

Well, the smile spreading across my face,
    I wanted to see on the whole human race,
So I rushed to take her hand,
"Come with me, Sweet Mary,

I'll take you home," I held her in my arms.

She whispered, "I am a Virgin,
But not the way they think,
It once meant we were autonomous,
    Not Sexless and Anonymous,
I want to dance in the world!"

We ran for the door
    her mantle unfurled
        And fell upon the floor,
And the weight of all
    those Darkened Ages
Was lifted from her shoulders.

She sparkled in anticipation,
    of her Sweet Emancipation,
No more lies about temptation,
The snake slithered from under her foot.

The Kundalini Current entwined us
    Both in Ecstasy,
And as we stepped into the street,
We turned back to hear the sound of feet,
And spied the old woman
        skipping quick and fleet,
    To catch us in our dance.

She said, "Mary! You forgot the Apple!"
We laughed and took a bite!

The Moon looked down on this Epiphany,
And bathed us in her light....
"Tonight, Tonight, is a Holy night,
  Let it never be forgotten,

When all the Pagans
        Danced for Joy!
And even Jesus, as a little boy,
Came home to Mary,
        When he beheld,
                The Moon beneath her Feet,"

So, Every day, Every church you pass,
Hail Mary! As she leaves the Mass!
Hail Mary! As she leaves the Mass!

## FOG IS A DEFINITE STATE OF MIND

I'm under-the-weather today,
And when you're under in San Francisco,
you can go pretty far down.
It's a strange kind of fog prison,
You know that 20 minutes in any direction,
Summer will be in full-swing,
and here you are,
freezing under a wet blanket,
that others dare to call rain.

People are known to go a little crazy.
We stay away from the Golden Gate on days like this,
unless we are feeling
we might derive some small pleasure from watching
the wind batter the tourists in their shorts and windbreakers,
Walking across a span
that disappears suspiciously into the whiteness
before they even get across.

There they are, searching through the mists
 for that other 'special' prison, Alcatraz,
and taking pictures that will seem utterly ridiculous
when they get home.
Don't get me wrong,
this has always been home to me,

ever since I hitchhiked up as a teenager,
out of the baking hot and boring flatlands of suburbia,
To dance and romp with the heads and freaks,
streaming through the city like light bulbs
on a Solstice Tree!

Harbingers of a joyous New Age!
(There, I said it).
We were peace warriors fearlessly placing flowers
in the guns
of ignorant men.

These rolling hills will always ring of freedom
and rock-and-roll!
Tucked in every hillside, alley,
and around every corner,
We move from world to world.
The man in the old-fashioned Zoot suit
beats my heart awake,
and turning,
I hear real jazz wafting up the Fillmore,
not that noodling, white, intellectual jazz,
Jazz you can dance to!

And winding up the hill,
Japantown plum blossoms,
offer a delicate bouquet of beauty
to breathe into.

Climbing the next great mound
up to North Beach and Chinatown,
Where we're still working out the power dynamics for sure,
But the food is fine, and the bars are loud
with politics and pundits.

Up here you can see Fisherman's Wharf,
It's good from a distance-
we leave that land mostly to the tourists,
unless we need their business.

Don't get me wrong,
We are always great hosts to those who come to visit,
that's why so many take refuge here.

Then swooping down to the financial district, that some
workers in these upscale mines, call Fi-Di.
Suits that never really unpacked their suitcases,
Nibble on what they think is cool in our culture,
just enough nourishment
to sadly keep them coming back.

But I smile when I remember Occupy,
in the midst
of the marketplace,
Where for months, we were wildflowers growing
through the cracks of late-stage capitalism.

Showing the miracle that an entire village can be created
within a matter of days in the belly of the beast.

Tent homes, kitchens, communication centers, a library,
childcare, anti-oppression think tanks,
consensus-based meetings about finally knowing
that every
voice matters,
Topped off with a march everyday to keep the
people awake!
And equality isn't something we manufacture we enact it
everywhere we assemble.

No one can wrench the dream of this new time from my heart,
For I have seen too many waves roll
onto the shores of this great city
and declare the rights of entire movements,
that were called insane all over the world.

Here our hearts will always be open and arms spread wide
to envelop the next ones who dare to self-create.
And we don't tolerate folks here, we celebrate them,
We're a queer folk for sure!

The Statue of Liberty allows them to enter
with a torch to light the way,
but then you're on your own.
Where tough guys dare them to make their mark,

Saying, "Come on in, you might have a chance, Give it
your best shot!"

But when you've made it all the way out to the Wild Side
West,
We are ready to love you for who you are,
not what you can do to prove yourself.
But you better damn well be authentic!
And ready to learn what it means to ride a Muni bus
Where 7 continents are represented;
where we are already all living together,
And Maya Angelou used to sit in the driver's seat.

We want the full reveal, nothing less,
Drag Queens, James Deans, Panthers, and Punks,
This ain't Broadway in lights, but the warmth of the Mission's
a'right,
Pagans, Poets, Preachers of truth,
with no religion,
or confession booth,
Find places to deliver their outrageous insights,
that spark discussions into the night.

We've marched for everyone, and if there's
someone we forgot, we're marching tomorrow
right into the rotunda of City Hall,

Where brides stare wide-eyed
as witches Hex the patriarchy
with laughter and cackles
and we demand, 'No more Prisons',
Break all the shackles!

We are restoring each other with love's therapy.
Stand in the circle of our magical hills,
throw away the pills that "don't do anything at all",
No matter what you've done,
There's always a way to come home,
in our City by the Bay...

## DANCIN' IN THE REIGN OF TERROR
*(Dedicated to Abbie Hoffman)*

Rich man you got your
                coat caught
                        in the door.
Driving your Jaguar
                hungry for more.
Drawing grids across the Earth,
Stealing Her abundant worth,
Hiding the mystery of death & birth
                safely in your churches.

The world lurches from your torture
Forget civilization we want culture,
        An organism that grows & knows
The Earth rejects the order of the WTO*.

Dancin' in the streets
Refusing the option of defeat.
We will not be your poor and huddled masses-
The real world has no upper classes.

You cannot pay us enough
        To scrub anarchy off your walls,
The music of the universe calls
        And we are dancing' in the reign of terror!
This land belongs to nobody

Everybody, Every body is her body.

The zero sum game
Is just a tricky name for greed trumping need every time.
    There is no rhythm, not any reason
      for the perpetual war killing season.

The reign of terror
Falls as the Trickster and the Wise Woman
Calls!
Calls us back to our own true selves,
sweeping the shelves of the marketplace
of all the plastics, poisons, and purposeless junk.
Come on Baby, Let's dance the funk!

This land belongs to nobody,
My body, your body, our bodies
Move and find the grooves
        in the groves of trees
      in the doves of peace
In the unstoppable rhythms of release!
Dancin' in the Reign of Terror
Make no error, Yes we can!
Si Se Puede!
Yes, we can!

*The World Trade Organization, WTO, met in Seattle in November of 1999. 50,000 activists converged on the city and blocked off all entrances, successfully shutting down this undemocratic, corporate-based entity that gave itself the illegal and immoral power to determine the destiny of entire nations, solely based on profit as the bottom line for all decisions.

## SUCH AN OLD, OLD WOMAN

New Mexico,
    No place to get your back up
                against the wall,
    So vast you'd better
                leave your past behind
And just try to deal.
It feels like your heart
                is being cracked open
                like a dry arroyo bed,
                like a gorge, begging
                for the soothing floods.
False seasons:
    Thunderstorms
        and hail
      Shock my sensitivity,
            Exciting my proclivity
                For the unexpected.

This land writes an expose
        on every soul that ventures here.
            No place to hide
                No handle,
Only the Candles of the Virgen,
        Flickering,
Licking the night sky,

   that chills you to the bone,
      won't leave you alone,
'til you dream
  Her Visions.

Decisions don't come
from reason here,
 They just,
    get,
       planted.
 Tenacious as cactus
    and won't
     let go.

I flee to los montañas
 For the soothing sight of water, trees,
But can only stay a while
  'til I slide down the side
       of her massive bowl.
Back
  into
    this flat furnace,
    this adobe oven,
Overseen by a coven of brujas determined to cook you
   'Til your marrow
      seasons the stew,

'Til all you knew
      to be true
dissolves in a heat mirage.
You are caught in a menage a tríos
            of flat, dry earth
            sweltering sun,
            and sky so big
You know you're in way over your head.

Big fluffy, frothy clouds
      Float by suggesting
        All manner of happy friends,
And...
   For a few hours
      The turquoise skies
      Open your eyes
             To a peaceful beauty...

But being lazy can mean death
      To the fool on the hill,
When clouds quick turn
      Into thundering Buffalo,
        Blackening the heavens,
     Herds bent on revenge
        Because they no longer
            Roam the Earth.

Every day a rebirth,
        Flowers
            out of dust,
Lovers shocked by their own Lust,
        But
            Don't
                Trust,
Just
    Stay
        Awake!
For
    Your
        Own sake,
Watch your back,
        Even the Godfather, himself
        Finds no corner for his feast.
Mafia men hide in the dark, cool
                      Caves
                      of
                      Casinos,
Thinking to steal a bit
            Of her riches
When no one is looking-
        But she is always looking!

Snake can take you in a second;
Slithering thieves find themselves
                                Crawling,
                                Craving,
                                No more the gold,
Just someone
    To take them in from the cold.

She will freeze you,
                Fry you,
    She never stops preparing new dishes,
She will even spice her cauldron
with your wishes,
If you pray real nice.
But don't think twice, don't hesitate,
    Or impatient she will fling her spoon
                To become the Moon
                      Of Lunatics,
    You a human coyote;
                Lean and longing,
            Begging for mercy,
Go to the river for mercy,
        Taste the water, Rio Grande,
        Take it like sacrament,
Burn the sage,

And let your Spirit leach into the land.
Only then will this cracked
                      And crazy Crone
    Leave
     You
     Alone:
Reveal her white sand thighs,
Her red dirt triangle,
Her brown skin hills,
                      Thrills you never
                          Thought possible
From such an Old, Old Woman.
She cackles
        at your foolish fears,
And suddenly,
          Like Frida, you are suckling
                          at her breast,
Turquoise tears
        Drop
        From your eyes,
A happy skeleton
  With
      No
          Disguise!

## I AM DEATH

I am Death,
I am here to tell all of humanity,
I cannot eat any more.
You are making me sick.
I am bloated, and poisoned
by the dead you dish up for me.

I have tasted terror in the meat of men,
dying before they lived,
shoveled off of battlefields
in foreign lands,
Saturated with uranium,
and peppered with pieces of cluster bombs
that break my teeth.

I do not seek your guilt and remorse,
I have none and I do my job.
But it used to make me feel satisfied
to feast on the full life of a loving, respected grandmother.
To taste the zest of a freedom fighter from Nicaragua who walked his talk.

To chew on the brain of a brilliant poet who died peacefully in her sleep.
These deaths made sense and I and my cronies composted

these past imaginations
into free floating energy of regeneration.

I refuse to eat the last of a species driven to extinction by
the greedy, grinding jaws of profiteers.
I offer this to a higher altar,
Where it is known that nothing ever sown is lost
forever.
I pray with bony fingers, and walk on.

But the very worst taste is of a mother who was beaten and
left to die, when she fought back at the border to save her
children.
Her ghost just hovers next to the corpse screaming, Why!
Why! Why!
Her face frozen in fear and disbelief,
Her grief unbearable, her red heart too beautiful to touch.
This you ask me to turn into soil?
Her cells will not release the memory,
She will spoil anything that tries to grow.

I am Death and you are killing me!
   "When do I get to eat organic?"

I am Death and I can take no more!
Before I slam the door between the worlds
let me offer you this pearl
My sister Life has come to speak
Listen, Listen,
   it is Her you seek!

## I AM LIFE

I am Life
and I see you,
"My people, you are so brave, so filled with dreams in
your hearts that you risk everything…
You have left behind your land, your language
the home of your precious childhood.
Driven out by the greedy ones that have come from the
North,
you walked a thousand miles.

I cannot think of a more courageous act then this.
To trust in a people to welcome you,
Because has not Lady Liberty promised to give everyone
a chance?
Because we all have a right to be free-
That's all you are asking.

You, like all your brothers and sisters before you,
will even take the hardest, lowest paying jobs.
You are willing to work long hours mopping floors,
or picking the crops in sweltering heat,
But now, not even this is offered.

Now there is nothing.
And still you stand, looking across the border
that runs through the middle of your hearts.
You, who are disparaged, called illegal, alien, criminal,
Still you rise!
And you are awakening hearts all over the earth!
You, my people are everything that is great about humanity,
I am Life and you, you are truly living me through your
fierce determination
to believe there is another way.

That there can be a day that is beautiful again.
That one day you will be warmed by El Sol
on the porch of your own casa,
And you will smile
with that sweet taste of freedom
          in your mouth."
    Sí Se Puede!

## THE RIVER

So many truths bubbling to the surface
of the fast moving River,
The language police can't burst them fast enough,
They think if words are reduced to sound bites
that all the soul will be sucked out of them,

Chew on this you syntax snatchers,
You want it pithy and to the point, we got that,
no problem,
Idle No More,
Black Lives Matter
No Justice, No Peace, NO Racist police,
Hands up don't shoot!

We are breaking the sound barrier
And shattering the doublespeak
Showing up the mindless media as pipsqueaks,
Peeking out from behind their
Iron Curtains,
One thing is certain,
The smelly, rotten, disease ridden
corporate body, that pretends it is human,
Pretends it has rights,
can't sleep at night,
can't live with itself
anymore,

It's played its final card,
Its last Trump
Selling for a Pence if your
still buying that shit!

Let's all just sit by its bedside,
Say goodbye to the corporate body,
the shoddy imitation of a life,
Lets pull the plug,
Ready, give it a tug.
The only juice that's keeping
it alive is our fear,
How will it all work without
someone pulling the strings?

Facing the unknown without answers
is the only way to get to know
the mystery,
History is definitely not telling the story!

So hospice, hospice, say goodnight
Goodbye to the lies that keep us separate from life,
Its death to corporations, and nations,
and the meager rations that the rich give the poor,
Goodbye! Goodnight!
Take the corpse out the door,
Let it be the Burning Man
On the desert floor!

Time for that Rainbow Gathering again,
All colors, genders, dark and light benders,
News Flash!
The traditional family just crashed as well,
sending condolences,
 now let love call the shots!

I'd rather dance on the corpse of the corporate body
Than let one more friend die at the hands of the greedy,
So damn it!
Let's govern ourselves, and bring out the plow,
Let's ready the soil with these composting corpses,
Plant the seeds of the new world,
    this moment right now!

Change is slow......bullshit!
Let's go!
There's no time like the present,
there's no time but the present,
Be kind, Be kind,
Be kind to ourselves and everyone else,
We never hated each other,
We are social fucking animals,
You're an animal; I'm an animal,
Wild and free so don't put no chains or handcuffs on another brother,
We'll just have to love each other back to life,

Are you ready? I'm ready!
And no, I don't know how
It's all going to work,
No, don't have all the answers,
But I know
The River's been flowing for a long, long time,
I hear the Universe singing and I want to Rhyme.

## ALICE WALKER

Today, I am looking into
    the face of Alice Walker,
The clear, expansive gaze
    of a woman
        who has looked deep
    into the well,
Who is alive to tell
    the story of her people.

After digging and digging
    in her mother's garden,
Refusing to be fooled
    by the white-washed fences
that said, "NO Trespassing!"
    Pushing past
    the endless shelves
    of white authors,

She reached back
    to find Zora Neale Hurston, a healer,
Pulling out the heart of her people
to show the world–
and delicately placing it back,
Intact and whole.

Alice wrenched her stories
out of a wretched past,
Refusing to wash them,
>	Fabricate them
>	or cut their roots off.

Alice you have pierced
>	the human heart of our times,
with the irrefutable truth
of an ugly secret:
Fear of the dark.

I am a white woman
>	looking into your gaze,
And doing everything in my power
to eliminate every trace
of my brainwashing,

Not just the knowledge
that slavery and prejudice are wrong,
>	that intellectually
>	and theoretically
I am politically correct.

I am meditating on
>	letting each stupid, separate fear
>	arise and pass out of me,
Like a disease when the fever breaks.

Thoughts like "How unusual to see
        such an intelligent 'negro'"
or "Why would anyone want to kiss
        those big, fat lips?"
Words echoed from my Detroit, white childhood,
Where 'colored' women could work, Oh! Yes!
as maids from dawn to dusk,
and piccaninnies, with their funny braids
attempting to tame that wild, "animal hair".

I am forcing a mirror to my face,
        tracing the curve,
        of your face
        with my eyes,
I am dropping my gaze in shame,
Knowing I live in a world
that gives me privilege to hate, to harm
those who I have been taught to perceive as other.

I want to eliminate
        the part of me
        that wants to pull you
            from your roots,
and give you token privilege
        so I can
        feel good
       about myself here
     where it is safe.

I want to exorcise
>> all the demons
>> of my programming
Until the little girl in me
reaches out to caress your beautiful
little girl hair,
And I ask you,
"Can I come play with you,
Will you take my hand, Alice,
Take me to the real freedom land?"

*Everyday we read stories about the tragic and unnecessary loss of life. This time I let myself be completely present for the truth in this very brief article about one woman whose life was stolen.*
*It is my intention to inspire you to do the same, so our hearts stay open.*

## HALIMA KHALIF IBRAHAM

The bullet entered the womb, the vessel,
    the holy of holies, the place of the mystery,
    and destroyed the life of the child.
The bullet entered this temple and took the life
of the mother, too.

The bullet, labeled United States Marine Corps,
was, according to officials,
    "fired as allowed by the United Nations
    rules of engagement".

The language of brutal murder is emotionless, sterile,
Perfected, to send Halima Khalif Ibraham,
    the pregnant mother of six, a poor tea-seller
    in Mogadishu, to a violent death,
As she washed her face in preparation for prayer.
Halima was not allowed,

by the United Nations regulations,
        to say a prayer that day.
Because a man from a rich country
was patrolling her street
        and decided he needed to shoot a man
        carrying a machine gun.
Then this innocent mother is caught in "friendly fire",
Another amazing lie of the master's language.

Everyone can say, "Oh! well, the other man
        had a machine gun
        so he had to fire," and walk away from
        this news item
        with a clear conscience.

But the reality is this:

Open your ears down the narrow streets of that city
        as the reality of her death sucks the air away
        and clutches at the hearts of her children.
        They scream and go numb, in pain and shock!
Listen and look, if you can, at their faces
As the blood is smeared across their lives forever.

Those six children, the seventh unborn,
        cry out to us,
To say the prayer their mother was not allowed to say,
According to United Nations Regulations.

## AUDRE LORDE

Magazine rack
Racked with
    falsehood in eye-catching colors,
Female fashion
    hiding perfected fascism,
The guise
    of the prosperous
hides all disparity.

Shiny slick
    they beg to be touched,
    to be bought,
    to be believed.
and Ms. Magazine,
    carried a headline:

"Audre Lorde
    in her own words"
Her last words,
    they were always her own.

How many of us
    own our words,
select them
taste them
    turn them over on our tongues

To release them only with
> the full knowledge
> of their purpose?
> Audre did.
Audre could do nothing other than.

Hand-picking
> with the experience
> that allowed no excuses
>> or delusions,
Hand-picking
> with the sensitivity
> of fingertips
>> that were bound to the promise
> "to leave no pen lying in blood".

Pressing words
> to know their ripeness
> or their rottenness
To labor endlessly
> not to be misunderstood.

To let no one mistake her meaning.
That no black sister
> will see her
> as enemy
For her love of women.

That no white sister
        will leave
        her work
        with only
                an intellectual grasp
that is still cold and pale as her skin.
That no black brother
        will accuse her
       of being a traitor.

No child deny she is a mother.

        In her clarity
Pain could not be ignored.
She would not soften
        the experience
        to our taste
                or waste
        a syllable in flowery prose.

And I suppose
        in this world racked
By Cold Cruelty and Greed,
She always knew that
        what we all need
Is a way by the Slick Trick
        in the cellophane wrapper,

A way by
> the categories
> that grow to
> wall us in

Where
> we are manageable,
> molded
> > and molding,

Rotten to the core
until we are willing to touch
> that core,

And speak no more

Until we open
And risk it all
To touch each other.

To Audre Lorde
> people were not hordes,

But chords, in harmony,
I want to be in harmony with you,
Audible, Audacious,
You, Audre,
You,
Sweet Lorde!

*Andy Lopez was only 13 years old when he was gunned down by Sheriff Erick Gelhaus in broad daylight while carrying an airsoft toy gun that many children were known to play with at this very sight on Moorland Ave, in Santa Rosa, California. Within seconds of arriving at the location Andy was shot 7 times, 4 bullets hitting him in the back. As he lay dead on the ground, he was handcuffed.*
*No charges were ever filed against Gelhaus. This poem was read at the Sonoma County Board of Supervisors to stand in solidarity with Andy's mother Sujey, all of Andy's family, friends and the community.*

## JUSTICE FOR ANDY

When a mother births a child,
She sends dreams of the future
into the world,
And when that child
is killed in cold blood,
all the dreams blow back
in her face with a gale force,
like a fire
out of the gates of hell.

All Andy's dreams now weigh
on his mother and father to fulfill,

and she is asking us to help her.

We are mothers and grandmothers,
we never want to experience
what Sujey is feeling.
But still when we hear the news of another child
dead at the hands of the state,
we must dip our toes into that fathomless,
dark pool of grief, to empathize, to bear witness,
but we cannot drown there,
nor let our sister, Sujey, drown there.

It is the worst nightmare of every mother
who ever lived, it is against the order of things.

And you hide Gelhaus behind you,
you let him continue to be silent.
You have shut down your meetings,
called out snipers and riot police,
scaring Andy's young friends, filled with grief and disbelief,
That their friend is dead, that a piece of them died that day, too.

A man, a man with dignity,
would come here and beg
for forgiveness,
own his actions,
look into the eyes of Sujey
and know the pain she is feeling.

You too, need to own your responsibility
in this travesty,
Own that our system is broken,
Own that you have served the rich,
while Latinos are called
Illegal, called alien,
Constantly living with fear and intimidation,
until what was unthinkable became inevitable,
The shocking finality of a murdered child.
You are afraid too,
afraid because
you know how wrong this is,
know that a wildfire of truth
a brigade of our youth,
will not relent
until Andy can truly rest in peace.
Until we together do everything in our power
to protect his friends and their bright and fragile futures.

We do not care about your
procedures, they have allowed Gelhaus to return to work
while a family
has a bullet hole through their hearts.

Grief creates a mighty anger,
Grief creates a fierce desire.
Grief creates a mighty fire!
that tears alone cannot extinguish.

## JUSTICIA PARA ANDY

Cuando una madre da a luz a un niño
ella envía sueños de futuro
al mundo
Y cuando ese niño
es asesinado en sangre fría,
todos los sueños soplan contra
su rostro con la fuerza de un vendaval,
como un incendio
salido de las puertas del infierno.

Todos los sueños de Andy ahora pesan
en su madre y su padre para que se cumplan
y ella nos pide que la ayudemos.

Somos madres y abuelas.
nunca queremos experimentar lo que Sujey
está sintiendo.
Pero aún así, cuando escuchamos la noticia de otro niño
muerto a manos del Estado,
debemos mojar los dedos de nuestros pies en ese insondable
pozo oscuro de la pena, para empatizar, para dar testimonio,
pero no podemos ahogarnos en él,
ni dejar que nuestra hermana, Sujey, se ahogue en él
Es la peor pesadilla que toda madre
haya vivido, va en contra del orden de las cosas.

y tú escondes a Gelhaus detrás tuyo
tú dejas que él continúe en silencio
tú has cerrado tus reuniones,
llamado a los francotiradores y a la policía antidisturbios
asustando a los amigos jóvenes de Andy, llenos de dolor e incredulidad,
Que su amigo está muerto, que un pedazo de ellos también murió ese día.

Un hombre, un hombre con dignidad,
vendría hasta aquí y rogaría
que lo perdonaran,
admitiría sus acciones,
miraría a los ojos de Sujey
y sabría el dolor que ella está sintiendo.

Tú también, necesitas admitir tu responsabilidad
en esta farsa,
admitir que nuestro sistema está roto
admitir que has servido a los ricos,
mientras que a los latinos se les llama
Ilegal, se les llama Extranjero,
Constantemente viven con el miedo y la intimidación
hasta que lo que era impensable se hizo inevitable
la finalidad impactante de un niño asesinado.

Tú también tienes miedo,
miedo porque

sabes lo malo que es esto,
sabes que el fuego incontrolado de la verdad
una brigada de nuestra juventud
no cederá
hasta que Andy realmente pueda descansar en paz,
Hasta que juntos hagamos todo lo que podamos
por proteger a sus amigos y sus brillantes y frágiles futuros

No nos importan sus
procedimientos, estos han permitido que Gelhaus regrese al trabajo
mientras que una familia
tiene un agujero de bala atravesando sus corazones

El dolor crea una ira poderosa,
El dolor crea un deseo feroz.
El dolor crea un fuego poderoso
que no se puede extinguir solo con lágrimas.

## CORONA COCOONS

Life just got too precious for words-
But I will try...
Looking out my window at the olive tree,
    branches free in the very slight wind,
The city is as silent as it was
when the sand dunes went on for miles,
    and Ohlone tunes still brought smiles
    to the women of the Tribe.
But now, like a movie showing
    the deserted streets of the bygone years
            of a fallen empire,
Church spires rise,
But inside the cobwebs grow,
    and the only sounds
        are echoes of a dying god.
and I guess I could cry for us all,
but I haven't got the tears.

Giant monuments to money scrape the grey skies
but not enough to let the sun break through.

Each in our private worlds now,
Meditation time is here, unbidden
but we have no choice.

I face myself, I face the wall,
but the window helps me remember
distances and everyone I love.

I see you all, my sisters and my brothers,
each of us caught at home in the spider webs
        of our own making.
 Seeing that all the taking we have done
        has won us nothing.

Now my heart beats like thunder wishing to be heard
but no one can hear it.
We hide and hurt and dream again
waiting for the day when rhythms of the outer world
call us to sing that forgotten love song
that heart-wrenching refrain.

Pain takes on new meaning when no one
        has tried to hurt you,
But the disease called Corona
is taking back all we owe to Mother Earth.
She is reveling in breathing without
        our poisons in her lungs.

Who knew the unsung hero would
be a virus to put us on the run.
And we are all eclipsed just like the Sun.

Moon Mama stands between us
        and asks at night,
Is this really the world you dreamed
when your bright eyes first gazed upon the world?

Yes, a Corona is the light that shines a crown
        around the black face of Hecate.
I never thought I would see the dark side of the moon.
The sun's light licks around her face and flares
        and tries to shine.
But it is not time yet,
        we have not metamorphosized.
        Each a separate journey.

We are caterpillars in our grey cocoons,
praying to let the darkness of our heartless
acts die and regenerate our imaginal cells.

We are either going to wake up
and fly like butterflies one day,
        or fear death as we travel
            in a gurney past
masked faces of compassion,
or detachment, or just naked fear.

If I could I would go
from house to house,
slitting open your cocoons

so everyone could fly again!
But none of us can free the other
We must rest, gestate and grow alone, an early release
and we will not have the strength to fly,
No one can crack the bird's egg or open our cocoons.

I wish at night upon the stars
that we can all recall the song that was born in our hearts,
remember the gifts we came to give so many years ago
and if we do the work of doing nothing,
a breeze may come one day and lift us to the skies.

We will look on Wall Street with disdain and
laugh at the war machines,
As we melt them into peace sculptures in every
field and park.
And praise the arts, not in museums,
but out in the Commons once again!

I hold you all so precious in the safety of my heart,
and yearn for the Monarch,
and the Giant Moth,
The Blue Morpho, lifting off in space.

The old human race is over.
No more laughing all the way to the bank,
No crushing flowers
with death-dealing tanks, let us be

a decent species.
Meanwhile, the pigeons own the streets,
And hawks and crows and murmurations of starlings
mock us with their freedom.

*As I looked at the photos of homes after the fires in 2017 in California, I noticed that what remained were statues of spiritual icons and hearths.*

## THE YEAR OF THE PHOENIX*

Fires rage through homes
licking the last taste of uneaten feasts,
photos floating through the air
landing somewhere, anywhere
looking for the eyes of remembrance,
that we are not just lost to the collective memory
of our existence.
Sacred hearths of brick and mortar
still stand with ghosts warming their hands all around,
Do you see them amongst the ruins?
Statues of the calm meditator, Buddha
chanting, "everything changes only love remains",
echo through the hollows of washing machines
and burned out car shells,
like giant insect hulls deserted.

St. Francis still beneficent, on the land of Marianne,
Praying for all our creatures
in flight and on the run.
Mary, always holding to the knowing

our hearts are good,
we are all innocent children within,
only needing love to thrive and be kind.
The humans have fled with their dreams
buried under nightmares of the uncontainable
power of fire.

We cannot fight the elemental forces
only call on them to hear our cries;
...let us breathe and bring the merciful
rains gathering from the ocean's depths
to form sheltering clouds of moisture,
...wet our parched lips so we may lovingly
kiss the earth and start again,
This time
leaving behind our warlike ways
in humble surrender.
Wings to the sky,
each of us a Phoenix,
seeking rebirth and one more chance
to love and dance on the sacred ground
of the mysterious Mother of us all.

*Phoenix is an alternative name for the Year of the Cock/
Rooster in Chinese Astrology.*
*4:03am October 12th, 2017*

*I've heard of a murder of crows and a school of fish, but when I learned of a parliament of owls, a poem came knocking at my door.*

## A PARLIAMENT OF OWLS

There they sat.
where no one saw them.
in the dead of night,
in the branches of the Redwood Ring.
They knew it was time,
it was almost past time, but not quite.
It was late, but not too late. It was time.
There could be no more omissions,
or religious missions, only emissions of the truth.

Breathing and birthing truth,
because what is under attack is truth.
Not The Truth, only fools and fanatics
believe in The Truth. Truth is not absolute.
It is resolute, it never goes away.
It is what starts our hearts,
and just has to go underground to survive at times.

Underground the truth is a matter of fact.
It is truth, that comes from a Ruthful heart.

Oh! Had you forgotten about that word,
Ruthful?
Me too,
I just found it again, dusted it off,
and started using it.
Ruthful, is to be full of compassion.

We have been stuck in the muck of a ruthless world.
And a ruthless world has no respect for truth,
    Truth that is rooted in common sense,
              in an ethic of the heart,
That does not pretend you can just make up any lie,
    then use it to steal from her beautiful body,
The body of Mother Earth,
    Gaia, She has many names.

The Parliament of Owls knows it is time.
They don't need to vote, there is no debate,
They know it is time to create an allegiance with the humans,
"They need us," said the eldest, and the youngest nodded.
"The women will listen, they are ready to receive."
They each gave a deep and resonant Hoot
and passed it round the Circle,
The Cone of Power was raised and it was time to take flight!

Silently, in the pitch black of night, they flew
To the town hall where the 13 Grandmothers were
Holding their Ceremony of Life,
Singing the songs of the Ancient Ones,
The songs of the Wise.

The Parliament entered the hall,
Circling the women and making eyes at each one,
Until each recognized their familiar.

Landing gently on her shoulder,
An Owl for every Woman,
They began to sing together,

Because it was time.
Time backwards is emit.
Time to omit nothing in the Song of Life,
Not even the Mosquito.
Time to Utter the Ruthful Truth.
That is all that is needed, that is all.

www.ingramcontent.com/pod-product-compliance
Lightning Source LLC
Chambersburg PA
CBHW070438010526
44118CB00014B/2090